# Everything You Always Wanted to Know About Kindergarten — But Didn't Know Whom to Ask

## Edited by Ellen Booth Church

Printed in the U.S.A.
ISBN 0-590-93602-8

2   3   4   5   6   7   8   9   10          02   01   00   99   98   97   96

# Table of Contents

**12.** How are art, music, and physical education part of the curriculum?

**13.** What will my child learn about getting along with others?

**14.** How should discipline be handled in kindergarten?

**15.** What role do special support staff and specialists play in the kindergarten classroom?

**16.** When should I talk to my child's teacher? When should I talk to the principal?

**17.** What can I do at home to support what my child is doing in school?

**18.** Why should I get involved with a parent group like the PTA?

**19.** How will my child be evaluated in kindergarten?

**20.** How can I tell if my child is ready for first grade?

### Plus ...

### A (baker's) dozen things
### to ask your child's kindergarten teacher

### 5 things to look for
### in the kindergarten classroom

# 1 What is the real purpose of kindergarten?

**Most American children go to kindergarten, but the kindergarten experience varies from school to school.** There are differences in the approach to teaching and learning, but there are some common goals among kindergarten programs:

- Perhaps most important is the development of self-esteem. This means helping children feel good about who they are so that they feel self-confident and competent as they continue in their schooling.
- Also important is the emphasis on cooperation: helping kids learn to work and get along with others.
- A common goal is fostering children's curiosity and natural love of learning: helping them learn to express themselves — to communicate and represent their ideas, feelings, and knowledge about the world through the development of their beginning reading, writing, math, and science skills.

The kindergarten experience provides the foundation skills for learning and thinking that will enable children to become enthusiastic lifelong learners — enthusiastic because they have discovered that learning is fun and meaningful.

## 2 How is kindergarten different from preschool? From first grade?

**The significant difference to your child is that kindergarten means going to "real" school and being a big kid now!**

The main contrast lies in the developmental expectations for each age group. Preschool and child-care programs help children learn how to play with their peers and interact with different materials, as well as separate from their parents. While play and socialization are also key elements of a kindergarten program, kindergartners are ready to be introduced to more formal learning and to work in a more organized, independent manner.

Developmentally, kindergartners are more capable of:

■ participating in extended group activities

■ planning and executing self-directed activities

■ engaging in symbolic play

■ researching ideas or questions

■ using beginning reading and writing skills for communication

■ applying basic math and science skills to life experiences.

In many schools, first grade means an even more structured approach to learning, with less emphasis on play and more on teacher-directed academic tasks. Some educators believe, however, that first grade should look and feel more like kindergarten — with an activity-based integrated curriculum that responds to individual developmental levels of young children.

# 3 What makes a good kindergarten program?

**A good program expands a child's ability to learn about the world, organize information, and problem-solve; in turn, this increases the child's feelings of self-worth, confidence, ability to work with others, and interest in challenging tasks.** Children should feel free to express themselves through language, drawing, and writing and through the use of blocks, paint, clay, and other creative materials.

A balanced program also includes a combination of formal and informal activities, investigations, and projects that allow children to work on their own and in groups.

Most activities are designed for small groups, with large-group activities requiring children to sit for limited amounts of time. Work is presented through an active, hands-on approach that incorporates children's interests and ability to apply what they are learning to meaningful life experiences.

An emphasis on developing the love of literature, reading, and writing should permeate the environment. Children are exposed to the written word through meaningful print around the room, books, charts, recipes, signs, and self-published books. Children are encouraged to participate in shared and independent writing activities.

The curriculum and classroom atmosphere should support the development of essential creative and critical-thinking skills: observation, prediction, experimentation, deduction, and making comparisons.

# 4. Are all five-year-olds "ready" for kindergarten, and what do I do if my child is not quite ready?

**No two children develop in precisely the same way or at the same rate.** Educators describe the child's development as having four different dimensions: intellectual, social, emotional, and physical. And they stress that these dimensions do not progress or develop at the same rate.

This means that some children may develop more quickly intellectually, while others progress more quickly socially, physically, or emotionally. All children are individuals who are growing, changing, and learning all the time.

Because different children develop at different rates, they are not all ready for all aspects of kindergarten at the same time. The best schools and teachers understand this and adapt their classroom plans to

accommodate the differences among children.

Historically, it was believed that it was best to give children an extra year at home if they were unusually immature or didn't seem quite ready to learn in a classroom setting. However, research shows that children benefit from attending programs that reflect their developmental levels and meet their growing needs, instead of programs that require children to fit narrow criteria.

The best programs meet children where they are and create a curriculum that serves everyone. Realistically, however, some programs may not be as flexible as others. Talk with the educators in your community's kindergarten program. You may be surprised at their willingness to look at your child's individual abilities and needs. However, if all agree that your child is not ready for kindergarten, ensure that there is an appropriate program she can attend during the year.

# 5 What happens during a typical kindergarten day?

**A good kindergarten program provides a varied schedule of active and quiet activities.** A predictable daily sequence helps your child feel secure and knowledgeable about the classroom. Yet, the schedule needs to be flexible enough to respond to the changeable interests and capacities of the children.

## Time at School

While many kindergartens are half-day in length, more and more are becoming full- or extended-day programs. Currently many children come to kindergarten with some previous preschool or child-care experience. They are ready, willing, and able to spend an extended time in school. Research shows that a full-day program can be less stressful for children and teachers because there is more time to spend on in-depth learning and activities. Often, a half-day program has to cover the same amount of work as a full-day program in — obviously — half the time!

## Sample Schedule

**Greeting Time**
arrival, sign in, looking at books, quiet games, free play

**Group Time**
class meeting, calendar, shared reading, writing, or math lesson

**Activity Time**
teacher-facilitated small-group activity, independent work in learning centers

**Outdoor Play**

**Lunch/Quiet Time**

**Storytime**

**Language and Literacy**

**Music and Movement**

**Closing Circle**
recall of day's experiences

# 6 What kinds of challenges might come up as my child adjusts to kindergarten, and what's the best way to handle these?

**Dealing with separation from parents, adjusting to a "big school," feeling at home, trusting the teacher, making new friends — these are all issues that kindergartners face.** The child who has been in child care or preschool — and had positive experiences there — may have an easier time adjusting to kindergarten than one who has never been away from home before.

But all incoming kindergartners (and their parents!) are encountering a new situation, which can cause some anxiety. Don't be surprised if your child — who was well-adjusted at preschool — suddenly seems less comfortable when suddenly surrounded by a big school, big school buses, hallways, a cafeteria, and older kids. Even having to spend more of the day sitting down may cause your child anxiety. And your child may have a hard time separating from you. A temporary regression in behavior and confidence is normal. Kindergartners aren't

sure whether they want to be "big kids" or stay little, so they will try both for a while. Be patient and supportive during this transition period when children are finding their identity within the new class.

Many parents and older siblings tend to talk up kindergarten as "real" school and emphasize concerns about discipline. This can cause fear in a child. It is important to talk about what might be familiar and safe in kindergarten, and not just about what will be new, big, and important.

To ease the transition, talk to your child in advance about what school will be like. Visit the school at the end of pre-school or during the summer. Before school starts, try to make sure that your child gets to play with another child who will be in the same class — both kids will benefit from seeing a familiar face the first day of school.

Together, decide on a special item or family photo to bring to school. And if you and the teacher agree that it will be helpful, you may want to stay in the classroom for a while during the first few days of school.

# 7 What does "developmentally appropriate" mean?

**"Developmentally appropriate" is a term you may hear applied to your child's kindergarten program.** It describes curriculum and teaching methods that are based on how children learn. If you have more than one child, you know that not all children learn skills in the same way or at the same time. This does not mean that one child is either slow or advanced; it simply reflects the different rates and learning styles of children. The core of developmentally appropriate practice (DAP) is this recognition that children's rates of learning and learning styles vary greatly. Instead of requiring all children to learn the same things at the same time, teachers who use this approach adapt their programs to fit the age and individual needs of each child in their class.

Some of the important aspects of DAP include:

- **EDUCATING THE WHOLE CHILD** — focusing on how your child develops in all areas: socially, emotionally, intellectually, physically, and creatively

- **INDIVIDUALIZED LEARNING** — reflecting your child's unique learning style, needs, and interests

- **INTEGRATED, MEANINGFUL CURRICULUM** — teaching early math, science, reading, and writing within the context of a theme and through hands-on activities that interest children

- **CULTURAL SENSITIVITY** — valuing the rich diversity of culture children bring to the classroom.

# 8 What is the role of play in kindergarten?

**When you are five, play is your most important work.** Children grow, learn, and even investigate the world through play — especially rich and complex play activities that allow them to solve problems and engage in fantasy.

Play is not something trivial that children need to grow out of. Instead, it is the basis for discovery, reasoning, and thinking. When children are given the freedom to experiment, to make mistakes, and then to learn from those mistakes, they are developing skills that will stay with them for life. When kindergartners play, they preplan, create a focus, and strive for a goal — essential life and work skills.

So, don't fret if your child comes home saying she played with the blocks all day!

You can be sure that your child was applying very important thinking, problem-solving, reading, math, and science skills.

In fact, ask your child's teacher whether there is plenty of time devoted every day to this purposeful play.

# 9 Will my child learn to read and write in kindergarten?

**That depends on your definition of reading and writing!** In the past, reading was defined as the ability to read word-for-word with few mistakes; writing as the ability to make recognizable letters and words. Current research shows that children use important reading and writing behaviors and strategies long before they can actually read everything on a page. Memorizing a book, reading the pictures to tell the story, predicting what will happen next, finding familiar words and letters, and even guessing are all important strategies that kindergartners use to make meaning out of text. Most children in kindergarten will use some or all of these strategies; however, kindergartners are not expected to read word-for-word by the end of the year.

A good kindergarten program immerses children in a literacy-rich environment in which the love of reading is key. Through literature, poems, charts, and their own writings, children find the purpose and pleasure of reading.

**Writing**

The new, broader definition of writing includes all strategies children use to express and communicate an idea on paper — pictures, scribbles, lines and spaces, letters, and invented spelling (using letters to represent a word in their own way). These techniques may not resemble what you know as writing, but your child may be able to read his writing back to you!

Children learn to write in the same way they learned to talk — through a string of approximations. Therefore, it is important to honor all forms of your child's writing, just as you celebrated his first attempts at speaking.

The kindergarten program should help children explore ways in which writing is useful and meaningful. To aid children's daily explorations with writing, the classroom should be equipped with a variety of writing tools — markers, pens, pencils, and crayons. Children should experience different forms of writing, such as messages, poems, signs, and journals.

# 10 What will my child learn about math?

**Children begin to understand numbers through measuring, comparing, counting, and matching quantities.** A kindergarten program introduces these concepts in activities with special hands-on math materials known as "manipulatives." These include construction toys in a variety of shapes and colors, puzzles, and small objects for sorting, counting, and classifying.

Regular building blocks are a great early-math material for exploring geometry, parts and wholes, patterns, and measurement. By using these "real things," children see the purpose and use of math. Their findings from weighing, measuring, and estimating activities are written or recorded on charts and graphs, thus providing meaningful experiences with writing numerals.

## 11 How will science and social studies be introduced?

**Young children are naturally curious. They are "born scientists"** who investigate and ask questions about the world around them: about the changing seasons; as they examine how things work; when they wonder how animals live; when they ask questions about life, health, and even space.

As children explore, they experiment, they invent, they think about cause and effect, and they predict results — all stages of the scientific method!

Children explore materials they are familiar with: sand, water, clay, and paint, among others. For example, as they use blocks, they discover the principles of balance and gravity; as they use sand and water, they experiment with volume and flow.

In kindergarten, these experiences are taken to a higher level of thinking by writing down predictions and recording and graphing the results of experiments on class charts and in science journals. These enable a child to see her ideas and findings in print and to share them with others.

**A good "social studies" program starts by looking at the lives and cultures of the children and their community.** This helps children understand and appreciate who they are, helps

them understand others, and provides a base from which to look at larger communities.

Culturally sensitive programs celebrate similarities and differences among children, building a child's sense of self within the larger view of the world and encouraging an understanding and appreciation of those who live different lives.

Children learn by using culturally diverse materials in all areas of the classroom, by looking at pictures, hearing stories, going on field trips, and just getting to know each other and other families. Activities and discussions are provided in the areas of conflict resolution, economics, relevant history, ethics, careers, and work.

# How are art, music, and physical education part of the curriculum?

**Art, music, and physical education should all play big roles in kindergarten programs.** In addition to giving children ways to express themselves and exercise their creativity and their bodies, they help build coordination (small- and large-motor skills) and develop literacy, math, science, and problem-solving skills.

Sometimes teacher "specialists" visit the kindergarten classroom. At other times children visit and work in specialized art or music rooms. In many schools, classroom teachers integrate art and music activities into their regular kindergarten curriculum, seeing the arts as a core from which many skills are generated.

The kindergarten classroom should have plenty of art supplies easily accessible for children's daily independent use. The classroom should be alive with music and movement throughout the day as children use simple instruments, sing songs, dance, and listen to culturally diverse recorded music. Art and music are essential to the literacy program, since they provide a myriad of opportunities to use language, reading, and writing.

The active play of physical education helps children build not only their strength and muscular coordination, but also their social interaction skills. Ideally, the school has an outdoor playground with equipment geared to small children. But some physical-education activities — such as fun dance and creative-movement games — work equally well indoors.

# 13 What will my child learn about getting along with others?

**A good kindergarten teacher helps children work in groups, play together, listen to each other, solve conflicts, and become sensitive to one another's feelings.**

Children learn important social skills and behaviors through their interactions in formal and informal activities. Developing social skills is crucial to success in later schooling, because children who cannot participate in groups find it difficult to listen and learn in large class settings.

Kindergartners are very social, and their relationships with peers are very important to them. These relationships can at times be very volatile. The teacher is instrumental in introducing children to methods for resolving their disagreements in peaceful and positive ways. Facilitating children's ability to problem-solve — in group time and independently — is a key function of kindergarten teachers.

# 14 How should discipline be handled in kindergarten?

**Generally, a positive approach to discipline is used in kindergarten — preventive actions rather than punitive reactions.** Teachers use techniques that anticipate problems, provide alternatives, set clear limits, and establish logical consequences. They explain the expected behavior by phrasing rules positively and giving directions clearly, rather than simply listing a set of "don'ts." They deal with a child's behavior rather than pass judgment on the child. Good teachers will monitor activities that may overstimulate children and propose ways to refocus inappropriate behavior.

It is important for children to learn responsibility for their own behavior. A good classroom setting encourages children to be part of the management system by including them in the development of classroom rules and in solving interpersonal and class problems. Interestingly, children can be the best monitors of their peers' behavior!

# 15 What role do special support staff and specialists play in the kindergarten classroom?

**Specialists and support staff typically provide a wide range of teaching services.** In some schools, subjects such as art, music, and physical education are taught by "specialists." In other schools, this term for support people refers to psychologists, social workers, and reading specialists. It is important to ask your child's teacher about the role of these resource professionals in your school.

Specialists working with children who are having difficulties adjusting or learning may conduct a range of testing with the children to evaluate their individual skills and needs. A specialist may also decide to seek additional information about how a child may best learn. As a parent, you should be consulted and give your consent before your child is tested. School psychologists often visit the classroom — as a matter of course or at the teacher's request — to observe what's going on, to see how the children are interacting, and to advise on unusual situations.

# 16 When should I talk to my child's teacher? When should I talk to the principal?

**When parents and teachers work together as partners, everyone benefits — especially the children.** To provide a complete program for each child, teachers need to understand how the child interacts at home. And of course, parents need to know what and how their child is doing at school.

To establish an early, positive link with your child's teacher, have a telephone conference or in-person meeting before the school year begins to introduce yourself and set up a partnership. Inviting the new teacher to visit your home helps your child see the teacher as a real person. Then keep communication going all year through regular conferences and school visits.

The principal will be most helpful on matters that go beyond the day-to-day activities of the classroom. For example, if there are issues to clear up about school policy or if you are seeking ways to get involved on a schoolwide basis, then you should not hesitate to see the principal. If your communications with the teacher have become difficult for some reason, the principal should be able to help you reestablish positive communication.

# 17 What can I do at home to support what my child is doing in school?

**The most important things you can do for your kindergartner are:**

■ **INCORPORATE READING INTO YOUR DAILY ROUTINE.**
Make sure that your child sees you reading. Surround your child with age-appropriate books, and read to your child each and every day. And read together: cereal boxes, road and store signs, recipes, maps, and the everyday print in your surroundings that has meaning to your child.

■ **PROVIDE MANY WAYS FOR YOUR CHILD TO REPRESENT HER EXPERIENCE.**
Encourage your child to write whatever she wishes — words, letters, or stories to accompany her drawings — in her own way and without criticism. Make use of the variety of language experiences in everyday life: together with your child, make a shopping list, write a telephone message, create a scrapbook or travel diary. Allow your child to express herself with paint, clay, blocks, and other materials, and encourage lots of questions. Remember, it's okay to make a mess— cleaning up together is an important learning experience too!

■ **SHOW INTEREST IN AND SUPPORT OF YOUR CHILD'S SCHOOL ACTIVITIES.**
Encourage your child to talk about school — without quizzing her — and show that you are *really* listening. Kids know!

**MOST OF ALL, JUST TAKE TIME TO TALK WITH YOUR CHILD.** Go for a walk together. Talk about what you see. Get engaged in the wonderful world of make-believe. Make up stories together. Your conversations will tell you a lot about your child's thinking.

# 18 Why should I get involved with a parent group like the PTA?

**Like all parents, you want the best for your children. You'll find that in order to have the greatest impact on your children's education, you need to work with teachers and administrators to support and improve your local schools and not leave the whole job to the professionals.** Getting involved with the PTA will give you a more active role in your children's education.

School boards and administrators are becoming more aware of "parent power" and are recognizing that the parent really is the child's first teacher. As a result, schools are increasingly seeking parents' active involvement and partnership.

The formal and informal interactions you have with other parents through the PTA will provide you with opportunities to share experiences and information. These experiences build a sense of community with other families that will last over the years. It is also helpful for children to know that parents are working together to make their school a great place.

# 19 How should my child be evaluated in kindergarten?

**Appropriate evaluation of kindergartners is a hot topic in early childhood education.** For many years kindergarten and first-grade teachers have fought against the use of standardized tests. These traditionally multiple-choice tests rarely show children's skills and knowledge of subject matter, but only demonstrate children's test-taking skills (which isn't even something children do in kindergarten). Unfortunately, these subjective scores were often used to decide whether a child was ready for the next grade.

The philosophy of developmentally appropriate practice has changed child-evaluation techniques. This approach uses a variety of sources for a more authentic assessment of your child:

- **ANECDOTAL CLASSROOM OBSERVATIONS BY TEACHER** capture a "snapshot" of your child's interests and abilities within everyday classroom activities

- **CHECKLISTS AND BENCHMARKS** show a continuum of progress in curriculum areas over a period of months

- **PORTFOLIOS** of children's work (art, writings, photographs, tapes, graphs, book choices) show what your child is capable of doing and will reflect her development over time.

Your child's teacher will share this information at a parent conference so that you have a multifaceted view of your child's experience in kindergarten.

# 20 How can I tell if my child is ready for first grade?

**It is important to emphasize once more that there is a very wide range of abilities and normal developmental differences among children ages five and six.** As a result, not all kids will be operating on the same level after one year of kindergarten. Do not assume that your child is not ready for first grade just because he seems to be less mature in some areas than other kids. It is important to remember that there is a great variability in children's speech development, physical coordination, readiness to sit still, and ability to relate to other children.

A school that uses a "developmentally appropriate" approach to primary education will have a fluid definition of what constitutes kindergarten, first, second, and third grade

work. Instead of being stigmatized as "failures" because they do not fit the school's definition of a first-grader, children are accepted wherever they are on a continuum of skills and behaviors across the grades. The first-grade program is then redesigned each year to meet the needs of the children in the current class. Interestingly, research has shown that developmental differences that seem very pronounced in the lower grades tend to even out by third and fourth grade.

Retention should be a very last choice for children because it can adversely affect academic achievement and self-esteem. Research has shown that holding your child back just to give him a head start in first grade is ultimately not beneficial. If your school is suggesting retention, talk with the teachers and administration about ways to accommodate your child in first grade — perhaps with tutorial or remedial help. Not surprisingly, retention has ramifications for the child, who may believe that she has failed and is being punished. It is essential not to damage a child's self-esteem or her excitement about learning.

In short, repeating any grade is a step to be taken only after serious deliberation by both parents and educators. And whether or not to repeat a grade is one of the most hotly debated topics among educators. Whatever your decision, it is crucial that you prepare your child emotionally for what will happen next and lend your full reassurance and support.

# A (baker's) dozen
## things to ask
## your child's kindergarten teacher

**1.** How will the children be welcomed to kindergarten during the first few weeks? Am I expected — or encouraged — to stay, or should I drop my child off?

**2.** If my child has some problems adjusting or needs some extra help, how will you let me know so that I can be part of the solution?

**3.** How many children are in the class? With how many adults?

**4.** What's the usual daily schedule? And how does that schedule form the basis of the curriculum?

**5.** How much time will children spend learning in groups, and how much time working independently?

**6.** How will you handle conflicts between children and discipline issues in the classroom?

**7.** What are the classroom rules, school rules, bus rules, playground rules? Is there an established school policy — or booklet — concerning vacations, emergency closing procedures, medical emergencies, and transportation policy?

**8.** How can I get to know other children in the class and their parents?

**9.** Will my child be given work to do at home? If so, how can I help my child?

**10.** What special events and field trips do you have planned? How can I participate?

**11.** If my child is not feeling well in the morning — or was sick the night before — when should I keep him home? What happens if my child gets sick at school?

**12.** What's the best way for us to keep in touch? How will I find out how my child is doing in kindergarten?

**13.** When can I visit the classroom? How can I contribute to your program?

# 5 things to look
# for in the
# kindergarten classroom

**1.** What is the room like? Does it have a book center, block corner, make-believe corner, art area, or plants and animals to care for? Do you see children's art and writing displayed?

**2.** What reading materials are available to the children — books, story tapes, oversize books? How about math materials (like cubes and pattern blocks) or science exploration tools and equipment (magnifying glasses, magnets, and sand and water table)?

**3.** What is the tone of the classroom? Do the teacher-student interactions demonstrate interest in and respect for children? Does the teacher create an atmosphere of acceptance for children's investigations?

**4.** Is there enough space for children to move around freely? To work and play in small groups and individually?

**5.** Is there an outside play area with safe, age-appropriate, yet challenging equipment?